In Plains Sight

MAP OF
TOWNSHIP 147 N., RANGE 79 W.
OF THE 5th P. M.

Scale 1¾ inches to 1 mile

WISE

Map of Township 147 N., Range 79 W. showing land ownership plat.

SHERIDAN CO.

In Plains Sight

BY BONNIE LARSON STAIGER

NDSU NORTH DAKOTA STATE
UNIVERSITY PRESS

Fargo, ND

NDSU NORTH DAKOTA STATE
UNIVERSITY PRESS

Dept. 2360, P.O. Box 6050
Fargo, ND 58108-6050
www.ndsupress.org

In Plains Sight, by Bonnie Larson Staiger

First Edition

David Bertolini, Director
Suzzanne Kelley, Publisher
Oliver West Sime, Graduate Assistant in Publishing

Book Team for *In Plains Sight*:
Jamie Askew and Sydney Larson

Cover illustration and design by Jamie Trosen
Interior design by Deb Tanner

The publication of *In Plains Sight* is made possible by the generous support of the Muriel and Joseph Richardson Fund and donors to the NDSU Press Fund and the NDSU Press Endowed Fund.

ISBN: 978-1-946163-26-4
LCCN: 2021933152

Printed in the United States of America
Publisher's Cataloging-In-Publication Data
(Prepared by The Donohue Group, Inc.)

Names: Staiger, Bonnie Larson, author.
Title: In Plains sight / by Bonnie Larson Staiger.
Description: Fargo, ND : North Dakota State University Press, [2021]
Identifiers: ISBN 9781946163264
Subjects: LCSH: Great Plains--Description and travel--Poetry. | Great Plains--Social life and customs--21st century--Poetry. | Nature--Poetry. | BISAC: POETRY / Subjects & Themes / Places. | POETRY / Subjects & Themes / Nature. | POETRY / Subjects & Themes / Family. | POETRY / Women Authors. | POETRY / American / General.
Classification: LCC PS3619.T3464 I5 2021 | DDC 811/.6--dc23

∞ This paper meets the requirements of ANSI/NISO Z39.48-1992 (Permanence of Paper).

For my children . . . and grandchildren . . . and theirs . . .

Contents

I. Grounding

Grasslands 3
You Never Get Used to the Wind 4
Ode to Barbwire 5
Yellow on the Willow 6
Coyote Comes Calling 7
Sprites in Morning Mist 8
A Force of Nature 9
Field Notes 10
When the Water Recedes 11
Owling 12
Wolf Moon Morning 13
Winter Still Life 14

II. Portraits

Welcome to Wise Township 17
Sepia Prints 18
Standing Ground 19
Roadside Memorial 20
The Waiting Room 21
Ice Cream Social 22
Line of Sight 24
Bakken Roughneck 25
Dear Kate 27
Judicial Temperament 29
Memory Care 30
Pear Tree on Highland Acres Road 31
Pendulum of Ordinary Time 32

III. In the Mirror

Sunday Morning Metronome 35
Terra Incognita 36
Shadowbox 37
Turning Heads 38
Chemotherapy Fields 39

Clouds on Parade..40
Hormone Replacement 41
Edge of Dismantling...42
Mistress of Millennia..43
An Aubade..44

IV. The View from Flyover Land
49th Parallel..47
Shuttle to Rockport by the Sea...........................48
Boylston Street Subway 50
Pilgrimage...51
Heading Windward from Horseshoe Bay.............52
Face in Her Phone..53
On the Way to the McDonald's Hospital 54
A Sonnet for Beethoven 55
Lesson in the Wine Cellar 56
It's All the Rage...57

V. Home Again
Four Minutes Fast..61
Where Have All the Clotheslines Gone 63
The Rabbit 64
Monday's To-Do List 66
Sun Cycle...67
Summer Trilogy..68
Decorations..70
Sisterhood of Pines..71
A Meadow for Monarchs 72
Surrendering..73

Acknowledgments and Notes
About the Author
About the Press

I.
Grounding

"Let it be about"

"Then let it be about"

Grasslands

Let it be about farmed fields
corn tall and wheat flaxen.
The edges of town fenced—
planted into mowed lawns.

S1

Sometimes it's about the plains.
Great Plains and high plains—vast
virgin prairies and short grass
prairies, grasses for grazing.

allit. *S2*

You know it all—the whistle
of wind through seed heads.
A whiff of sage in the air from
nowhere. Sometimes it's a deep

S3

tangle of roots below ground
or a thatch of sturdy stalks
crisp underfoot—revealing
what you didn't see yesterday.

asson. *S4*

Then let it be about grasslands
Unfenced—wide as the dome of sky
corralled by earth's curving. Then
we see everything and nothing.

S5

You Never Get Used to the Wind

Babies swallow their breath as the wind
    scrapes their faces and children grow up
    leaning into endless pressure against their back

Storms steal life from calves in spring
    the third day of wind carries
    thunderstorms of summer

Gales strip skin of prairie grasses
    eat the fragile soil and leave the bones
    of buttes exposed and sun-dried

Gusts plaster brown leaves against the Fates in fall
    bring blizzards on an angry tirade
    or a Chinook to melt the snow on a whim

windy form

bucolic

Ode to Barbwire

Praised be those bucolic prairies
perfumed with sweet clover
that secret meadowlark nests.
Wires stretched taut meander
parceled plots that keep livestock
contained to graze and laze.

Wedged between roads
paved with dust those twisted
strands disguise a cruel quest
to kidnap giddy tumbleweeds
until the switching wind
demands release.

Pity rambunctious calves
and spirits who gallivant unaware
into a tangled trap that snatches
a flippant paper bag,
a farm boy's shirt, and impales
another careless Cooper's Hawk.

strange line

3 Stanza
6 lines each

anthropomorphic "careless" hawk

Yellow on the Willow

standing on the corner of 4th and Shady Lane
       you barely give us a few days
       maybe a week

to notice your pregnant branches birth
       albino sprouts craning their necks
       with mouths agape

feeding on sunlight before you conjure
       the lace of leaves and simmer
       in summer's verdance

alliteration

Coyote Comes Calling

I am the four-legged
echo of the moon.
Hear me yip and howl
biting at the wind.

Remember that day eye-to-eye
I startled you picking Nanking
cherries in the shelterbelt
too close to my pups.

You know me
from the fresh bobcat bones
I left for you in your pasture.
I know your every move.

You sense me lurking
around your yard in the dark
hunting skunks who
forage in your trash.

Feel that chill up the back
of your neck. That shudder
when I'm too close but
you don't know why.

Yes, I know you. You can
almost smell my shadow.

Sprites in Morning Mist

On the shoreline's deckled edge
reluctant fog surrenders

strange An elfin halo tangos
with the lake's glassine surface

Miasma spurns
the sun's burning advances

A Force of Nature

On the High Plains we get all kinds.
One is a faraway tumble that cascades
over flat-topped buttes like the slow rumble

of tuned tympanies in the rear of the orchestra.
Eerily reassuring and uncountable.
Then there's heat lightning

harmlessly hopping cloud-to-cloud
after days of swelter—and bragging rights
of frying eggs on sidewalks. Also uncountable.

And then—then there's the angry god storms
that turn a sky the sickening green of angleworms
we squish after the storm passes

and the acrid smell of ozone
lingering like gunpowder.
Those are head-for-the-basement

gully washers—the likes of which would make
Dorothy and Toto take cover.
Then we must count—from the frightening flash

till we hear the clap and feel the concussion.
Each second a malevolent mile away.
Torn between running outside to see what's coming

when the sirens scream or watching the radar
incessantly blink the color of dried blood.
And once in a while—there's a sweet-tempered

surprise of thundersnow that murmurs
in a silent night of winter.
Did you hear that?

Field Notes

The afternoon began
a deep follow to the Missouri.
A field of late harvest sunflowers
stood persevering
shoulders hunched against
freezing drizzle—turns
into a snowfield overnight.

As if the morning wept snow
whittled furrows of dark
dirt—all that remains
of a search for the streambed
struggling to swell again
to accept the sorrow
and surrender to the river.

When the Water Recedes

along the upper Missouri,
what remains is ice.
When I say ice, I don't mean
a serene skating rink painted

on a Hallmark card. I mean jagged,
ice jam shards like a pileup
of 18-wheelers, flatbed trailers,
and mangled Mitsubishis.

When I tell you it's cold,
I don't mean windchill warnings,
put-on-long-johns, a-heavier-jacket,
leave-the-car-running cold.

I'm saying risk-amputation-
from-frostbite freaking cold.

Owling

Wolf Moon's crisp shadows
mark midnight on New Year's Eve
Great Horned Owl pumps one
silent wing flap to launch its
nightly ritual of stealth

Wolf Moon Morning

January's white space closes in.
I drudge outside among light pillars
tuck chin into shoulder as frost
leaches to my crumpled brows.

First light is the blue of skim milk.
I trudge in someone else's footprints
a half-step longer than my stride.
Plodding in the crunch of last night's

snowstorm and nature's reckoning,
I grudge against frost biting my face,
a foe whose half-truths are death threats
disguised in sub-zero suffocation.

Winter Still Life

The Farmer's Almanac was right.
            February is cold and wet
with occasional freezing drizzle.
            Meanwhile, the coffee is hot

here in my pre-dawn kitchen. Time to notice
            how winter winds defer to a sky
overhead begging to chisel hoarfrost.
            Overheard high in the cottonwoods

a pair of Great Horned Owls whoo and coo
            a duet before they sleep away
the coming day. Ice lace drapes the clothesline
            suspended in night's sequined necklace.

Without warning, an impatient Alberta Clipper
            sweeps across the Plains.
The house creaks and shudders
            as it braces against the wind.

The furnace fires to cut the chill.
            Time to pour a second cup while
tormented branches snap and crystals scatter,
            lost in the pillowed yard.

Pine boughs fat with frozen tears
            crush snow covered grass.
The Morning Star shrouded
            by her threadbare veil.

II.
Portraits

form

blue-assed

Welcome to Wise Township

Take the section line north to the "T"
      then turn east on Three Rusty Car Road.
Yes, one is a '42 Hudson Coupe.

They've been here longer than we have
      but not by much. You'll see our place
from there. Come on in, the door's open

and the coffee's on. Sign the guestbook
      and you're no longer company.
The kitchen cupboard doors are glass

so you can see to make yourself at home.
      Don't mind a few blue-assed flies
dead between the windowpanes.

We don't notice that stuff anymore. Later
      we'll head west on the two-tire track trail
to count our harvest of hay bales.

t, t, t, t

In the morning we'll cook pancakes and bacon
      on the griddle Dad made from a Maytag
washing machine lid. If the weather holds

we'll take a moonrise boat ride around the lake
      then lean back and watch the Northern Lights.
Of course, you can talk to the stars.

*conversational
slightly
prescriptive
tone*

Sepia Prints

A brittled box of a family's lives
distilled into vignettes.
Names, like a small town
newspaper, grow faint.

Homesteader stories
tell of leaving the home place
to find work in Bismarck. Tales
more vivid than true.

Depression stories.
See them pose. So many left
to find fortune or just hope
for work out West.

Drought stories.
Maybe oil bust stories.
Write if you get work,
those left would say.

Memories jaded by survival.
No photos of them leaving.
Faces fade like passing ghosts.
They never came back for good.

Standing Ground → *but leaving...*

somewhere in North Dakota 1890

He left his bride out East. Said he'd send for her after
he claimed a homestead and built a proper house,
had a good harvest and tilled a garden plot for her flowers.
Said she should take the train to join him. He didn't tell her

he claimed a homestead in a county named Stark and built
a two-room sod and sandstone house—then sent word.
She took the train to join him. He didn't tell her
the tracks ended in Bismarck. The last 100 miles by buckboard.

Betrayed, a sod shack—both house and barn waited for her,
fields of rocks, a meager harvest and a couple mangy cows.
Train tracks from Bismarck and 100 miles by buckboard
seemed forever away, but when the snow melted, she walked

miles across his fields of lies, past one remaining cow.
Last year's hailed-out harvest and her garden razed by rabbits
seemed forever away when she walked—all those years ago.
Left her husband out West and didn't tell him she was pregnant.

quatrains

Roadside Memorial

In the dairy aisle
her cart as a cane carries
six eggs and three white
picket crosses each lashed with
a tangle of plastic blooms

Near dusk she drives north
to the place where it happened
she kneels in the ditch
and stands the markers propped with
arthritic stones from the farm

Love this

The Waiting Room

honoring Becky Quanrud

My watch starts now
among friends taking turns.
Her room becomes the vigil. At 93
she rests unmoving between crisp
sheets, in a railed bed. The incessant
metronome of the IV's drip, drip,

drips and the wheeze
of an oxygen monitor tethered
by a tube in her nose. Like a sentinel
at attention, it counts her labored
bricks of breath and beams
her vitals to the nurses station.

The long hand tick, tick, ticks
toward mid-day, when the monitor
goes flat as she departs. Her essence
escorted away from the fray,
a perfect commotion of slack bellows
and veils of ancient muslin.

Now silent, her room
a floating island, someplace
between here and where.
Outside, a nurse
has tucked a simple placard
of a dove above the doorway.

Ice Cream Social

I attend each year wearing faded ennui.
Foamy ice cream, donated cake
the smell of urine stronger

than the coffee. I sit with Mother
at the end of a table that suddenly
seems too small.

Two men are wheeled in unwilling
or unable to be sociable. Dignity
left behind in their rooms.

An aide plops loaded plastic plates
in front of them and walks away.
One man, too young and aware

wears an Army t-shirt, camo shorts,
Nikes and a wheelchair.
With a flimsy fork he stabs at the cake

then tries bare hands. Frosting
lands in his lap. No one sees
and no one tries to help.

The older man strains to eat,
unaware, in his too-big khakis,
a work shirt, and a wheelchair.

His plate inches toward table's edge.
Cake flops to the floor.
Thinking another meal is done

he rolls himself away. No one sees
and no one moves to help.
Once again, Mother introduces me

to the woman who always wears
lilac perfume and a polyester dress.
So nice to meet you, I say

as the Lutheran Ladies
Chorus starts to sing
What a friend we have in Jesus.

Line of Sight

I forget when I first knew my mother was sick
      Doctors misdiagnosed multiple sclerosis and said she had polio
I forget when I knew there would never be brothers or sisters or
      when I stuck my tongue out at people who stared at her stumbling gait

I forget the first cane and helping Dad make her first brace in the garage
      The hammered thwack of a bolt through the heel of her Penaljo pumps
One by one her dwindling china teacups replaced with mint green Melmac
      The uninvited smell of bleach at every birthday party

When did I start hating her for the things she could no longer do
      then aching to spoon myself beside her bedridden body
I forget she hated the things she could no longer do
      and having no answer when she would ask, *Why me?*

I forget she could see our house from the nursing home
      just beyond the family plot at St Mary's
I remember now. Isn't there a law that restricts building
      a nursing home in view of a cemetery?

Bakken Roughneck

Yeah, I got me to North Dakota—hired on as a roughneck,
the most dangerous drilling job but the money's sweet.
I came scouting for work, others just lookin' for trouble.
After twelve-hour shifts for fourteen days straight on the rigs
I get twenty-one days off. Puts the sweet back in crude.
Time enough to rest up and head home

from the Bakken to Bakersfield or wherever is home
this year. Back there I knows a different kind of roughneck,
Ne'er-do-wells, my mama says. Street life is crude
so I left all that to make it right by my woman and sweet
kids. Send them my paycheck from working on the rigs.
Besides, too much cash around always gets me in trouble.

I spend my nights hoping she stays out of trouble
too. Prayin' she's taking care of the kids—safe at home
eating dinner, tending a homework assignment rigging
up some science experiment, or playin' roughhouse
with them in the yard. I imagine Momma baking sweet
rolls for the whole bunch on Saturday in her crude

Hotpoint stove. I remember when she called me crude
for not taking off my cap in the house. Talk about trouble!
There we live as if wishes were horses and life is sweet
until I'm back in the oil patch, then the crew camp is home.
I'm bunkin' in Building B with a hundred other rednecks.
We're bussed each shift to a well site to work the rigs.

Each mornin' we pass 'em on the way to the rig:
families in campers and tents in the city parks. Those crude
conditions are worse come winter. It's a rough neck
of the woods. I watch them older kids left alone and in trouble.
School kids bussed from places no one should call home
and I wonder if my kids' lives are any sweeter.

I know this dangerous world is far from sweet.
Out here, some po' fool dies every few months in a rig
explosion. Lucky if anything is left to ship home.
Once I found a guy's boots—his feet still inside. A crude
end to my shift and a helluva way to die. I was troubled
by nightmares for weeks. Just another day in a roughneck's

life but long as roughnecks keep pumping the Bakken's sweet
shale, I'll try keepin' outta trouble working on the rigs.
Maybe life is crude but I just keeps sending money home.

Dear Kate

I'd write you a poem that sounds like a letter
~W. H. Auden

Some crazy luck cast us
together in Room 222
mistaken for sisters—co-eds
        wearing matching
                Sassoon hairstyles

and sorority blazers then—
we mark another year
of unremarkable birthdays now
        memories
                on rewind

English majors—we became
teachers then corporate somethings
but always poets corresponding
        always living
                miles apart

I wonder—should I send you a note
along with a few poems
maybe something quick on the
        computer
                no—handwritten

Yet my best cursive
penmanship never could
compare to your chiseled letters—
        an ocean crossed
                with the strong strokes

of your fountain pen and nib
your signature swells
over me like the tides
        lunar tugs
                through years

leaving shells on the beach—
little notes to gather in my hands
and store safely away
        in a ribboned heart
                satin box

Judicial Temperament

for Justice Carol Kapsner

Her sedate chambers lined floor to ceiling
      with oaked rows of uniformed law books
      old leather seasons the air.

By the windows stacks of case files wait
      their turn to soldier their way
      through hours of briefs.

Behind the door—ready to shatter the silence
      her ceremonial black robe is upstaged
      by a swing coat in vibrant aubergine.

Memory Care

who cares for the bewildered minds lost
     in the rubble of cognitive chaos
parked bumper to bumper adrift
     in the hallway between
fragments of their dementia years

who walk a painted corridor of floor tiles
     like a record player arm scratching around
from nurses station to the locked supply room
     with circuits interrupted by snacks
of apple sauce and decaffeinated coffee

geriatric gentlemen brush away
     phantom strands of spider's silk
from vacant faces and finger
     mother of pearl shirt buttons
like well-worn rosary beads

lipsticked ladies in their nineties
     rock dollies and cry for Mama
wear homemaker hands
     and empty aprons crocheted
by church women who meet monthly

as the Loving Hands of Home Circle
     who cares for the agitated souls
spinning on a tilted axis of disorientation
     disremembered minds grown porous
fluid and leaking

another day another family comes
     and goes in their fog of hollow grief
to hear the same someone say
     who are you and why are you wearing
my wife's clothes?

Pear Tree on Highland Acres Road

for Linda Chapman

Before your tree blossomed
last spring   you left us
          and summer   to carry on.

Petals came down in clouds
of crushed velvet   lost in grass
          and sorrow.   Now those

burgeoning branches gift fruit
sunshine in the void.   As juice
          drips down   my chin

a flashback urge to turn back years
to call and ask you   who checked
          on the children last.   Were they

riding trikes between our yards
or slurping Kool-Aid   in the shade
          of cool blue   spruce limbs.

I blink myself back into today
children grown   kids of their own
          and damn   you are still dead.

Pendulum of Ordinary Time

The cock's crow heralds first light
                on a mother nursing her newborn
and down the road it wakes
                a grandfather's wizened fingers.

Time tenders pot-roast
                and potatoes under a cast-iron lid
infusing Sunday afternoons
                with onions and newsprint.

It overhears geese honking
                overhead as they wing southward
through the night—migrations
                of a thousand years.

Time sands over moments
                and decades soften like waves
vanish into shoreline—passing
                at the speed of Wednesday.

III.
In the Mirror

Sunday Morning Metronome

From my writing chair cornered
between French doors and winter
closing in, a load of laundry
languishes in my Kenmore washer.
It waits for me to slipper downstairs
to schlep its soggy worm-twist
of bedding into the yawning dryer,
its hot breath programmed to exhale
in cool-down cycle.

Blue-jean rivets tap dance
in a monotonous circle
around the cavernous drum
as I trundle back upstairs
contemplating next week.
I pause to peek through shutters
hoping to rescue the news
flung hard by The Kid
against the storm door. It's
now nestled on the stoop among
the first snowflakes of fall.

With one fleece-covered foot
tiptoed over the threshold,
I snatch headlines and retreat
as a gust rudely blusters past me.
The smell of fresh snow rushes inside
to fold newsprint and fabric softener
into aromas of toast and espresso.

The afternoon calls not for planning
next week but for storing summer
tools and finding snow shovels.
Meanwhile, my pen waits
to make a thing of them all.

Terra Incognita

There is no greater agony than bearing
an untold story inside you.
~Maya Angelou

Outside, rain pearls the pergola
and soddens Saturday's spirit.
Melancholy sinks into my bones.

Haunted by fading fragments
of unwritten verses held
prisoner behind a scrim

of my neglect. I mourn vaporous
voices, unreachable. Their faces
waiting to cross no man's land.

Frost forms.
Time hardens.

Shadowbox

November's hollyhock stalks
clack hollow against
each other in the wind

Inside the only sound
is my looking through
blued swirls of a puttied

pane mirroring my doubts
and practiced poise collapses
like a marionette

tangled in a diorama
of paint chips
dead flies and dust

Turning Heads

> *. . . you have discovered that being invisible is the
> biggest secret on earth,
>   the most wonderous gift anyone could have ever
> given you.*
>   *~ Mary Ruefle in* "My Private Property"

When we found ourselves at a certain age
        my friend asked, "Did you notice when
        you became invisible?"

Gone are the times when a certain sequined dress
        or a runway-walk in spectator pumps
        would own a room.

Done with false selves masking uncertainty
        each day a piece ascends
        wingless into unimportance.

Now I wear a certain *je ne sais quoi*
        and yes, perhaps I am unseen
        but have ceased to care.

Chemotherapy Fields

Nurses infuse poison into my vein
icy heat starts a killing spree—
barbaric cocktail meant to save.

News interrupts my steroidal numbness
targeted towers crumble—people
float slow motion to their deaths.

Another jetliner crashes
in a field nearby. Three pin-point
dots tattooed on my chest—targets

in a field of radiation. I question
my breast—did it conjure this cancer?
Welcome this alien invasion?

Back home, dirty blonde and gray
fall in clumps—drift like tumbleweeds
across my field of flax.

Clouds on Parade

I keep watch on the skies
  for thunder-bumpers building

mostly silent but sometimes
  they speak in tongues

stratus strands of wool
  carded & corded

woven & wefted
  with skeins of geese

Some days blades of cirrus
  slice the sky

give chase to their warring foes
  while I defer to those

gauzed ghosts pausing to greet me
  as I join them

Hormone Replacement

You used to torment me
     with impulsive
demands for attention.

Surgery, chemo,
     and radiation
insure meno-
     pause, and your lunar
pulses wane.

I declare liberation.
     You are discharged
to indulge me now.

Edge of Dismantling

. . . to see if I would go
or change into something else.
                ~Galway Kinnell, "The Gray Heron"

In a stroke of evolutionary voodoo
like casting off old selves
who bear no resemblance to you.

Parodies in ill-fitting regalia
you have been loath to abandon.
The sky slides into inked water

a murky sludge reaches up
from the aquifer to transform you
an ancient throwback.

a lizard in leathered skin
basks in the heat of the day
as though awakened

from shedding the past.
Now wears an avian costume
a heron feathered in a charcoal coat

appears like sweetgrass
arcs along a lazy lake.
Reedy legs high step lapping water.

Mistress of Millennia

Feet planted firmly in the ground
with roots of the cottonwood

This place is me—arms embrace
buttes and shelter young eagles

fingers smooth rough edges
of fieldstone over the ages

blood pulses down arteries
of the Missouri River

Aurora Borealis hair
streaks flaxen across night sky

North Star my guide—I ride
North Dakota wind my steed

An Aubade

I steal about before dawn
careful not to wake
the no one else
who lives here.

Saving daylight
I revel in the act
of awakening my senses.
I set my clocks ahead
hoping to vast forward.

IV.
The View from Flyover Land

49th Parallel

> Sweet Earth,
> Do you feel the boundary man has cut?
> Does it pain your prairies to be girdled so?
> With passports handed over and back
> we stitch the wound.

Shuttle to Rockport by the Sea

after Elizabeth Bishop's "The Moose"

As the plane taxis into Portland's terminal
I'm giddy for a Norman Rockwell ride
northward along Maine's serrated seacoast

far from my landlocked Great Plains
I've spent all day leaving

My instructions say the shuttle driver
will meet me by the baggage carousel
and there he stands holding a placard
flashing my name as if I am some dignitary

Grab your bag, dear, and I'll get the van
I'll be drivin' a gray Honda Odyssey

As we head up Highway 1 my vision
to drift in soft focus fades in a clatter
of his chatter and a touchy transmission

Wistfully I watch a 400-year-old shipyard
dissolve out the rearview mirror as forests
thicken and sugar maples saunter by

We rumble past foreign-looking
New England farmhouses awash
in timeworn shades of the tides

We thread through seaside villages
with church steeples piercing their heaven
and I lose count of lobster shacks beside
inlets with fury river fog rising

A gray odyssey indeed as I watch for dusk
to filter through primeval pines hoping
for a moose to meander onto the road
so we might pause in her magnificence

Boylston Street Subway

Into the gaping whale's mouth
      I fall. Stainless steel teeth
chew me and other morsels.

Carried by gastro-
      intestinal juices
Pushing and squeezing

through the blackness to a place
      I do not know
coming from a place I do not know either.

I appear into sunlight
      no worse off
than Jonah.

Pilgrimage

The Vietnam War Memorial
~Washington, DC

Rising as a stealth submarine
from the ground to a peak
then submerging. A sleek black
counterpoint to the aging columns
and shrines to dead presidents.

We are both here, strangers to this place
and to each other. He was the father
to one of the names. I was a blithe co-ed
at first untouched and unaware
of the growing list of names.

We both weep as we pace
along the cobbled walk
separate yet together
overcome by the stacking
of row
upon row
upon row
of names.

Heading Windward from Horseshoe Bay

A thick smell of diesels
        drones off our stern. Tourists,
we sail under the maple-leafed flag.

A sliver of glass and steel, Vancouver
        dissolves at dusk in our
bubbled wake and harbor fog.

Rainslickers issued as we came aboard
        tuck faces away from pin-pricks
of mist on our numbed-red cheeks.

The captain steers into September.
        The scent of ancient cedar
welcomes us across the starboard bow.

Face in Her Phone

White tails, ears perked, they stand watching
Her amble down a northern Minnesota road
In a hoodie against the damp—she's unaware
Three does are a mere twenty feet away.
Engrossed in her walking head down,

They don't seem bothered or move to safety—
A thicket of shoulder-high brush nearby.
Instead they follow her with synchronized eyes,
Like supporting cast in a silent movie.

Dappled beside the curtained backdrop—
Elegantly choreographed, yet she misses this
Early morning wonder—lost to her own
Rambling texts about a meet-up at Starbucks.

On the Way to the McDonald's Hospital

Abbott Northwestern
~ Minneapolis, MN

Two egg McDragons
tattooed on her muffin
top. Exploratory people
watch surgery. Waiting
room strangers patient-
ly lie about the weather.
Piano plays The Entertainer
sans player.

Disorderly orderly
assists a walker with a walker
jabberwocking laps
to the golden arches
and back but nurses
say leave the gown open
in the back. *Do you*
want fries with that?

A Sonnet for Beethoven

In the corner, past the burl-framed landscapes
and portraits hung in the art gallery,
a pianist as background ambience
begins to play your Moonlight Sonata.

Compelled by your symphony I ribbon
a path across the room through a loud crowd
nattering around sipping chardonnay.
Beyond patrons unaware, I arrive

at the grand piano. The lid raises
and I drift inside. Surrounded by strings,
basswood, the timbre of the master's piece,
music and moon shadows, I am welcomed

into a grand sanctuary, meeting
melancholy dressed in mahogany.

Lesson in the Wine Cellar

Tucked in a cool corner
of the Abbey's foundation
of rough-hewn granite
Abbot Robert offers a taste
of vintage cabernet

and explains the need to purge
oxygen from the bottle
keeps the wine from turning
He said, *purging has lots of uses
in the wine business*

*Once in a while
it's good for people too*

It's All the Rage

I am not a political activist
nor am I disenfranchised
or without opinions
or seeking a platform
from which to wail or rail.

I am an obscure Plains Woman
easily dismissed and swept away
by the contrails of flyover folks
in the red-eye sky.
I am a brave descendant

of survivors abandoned
by coastal elites
on a stubborn land
of old souls
among old stars.

V.
Home Again

Four Minutes East

Fall settles on the prairies
winter waits on the wings
of a million migrating geese
passing through. Geraniums

discarded on trash pick-up day.
Porch furniture stowed
beside rakes traded reluctantly
for shovels and ice melt.

The mind plays tricks this time
of year like "what if I blow
this pop-stand for a place
to wait out the winter—someplace

tropical and a rainy season—
that dampens afternoon's swelter
and inspires a men's chorus
of exotic bullfrogs?" Maybe

I'll give my neighbor a key
get on a plane and fly far enough
away until no one at my destination
has ever seen sleet, much less snow.

With a leap in logic, imagination
drops me in Malaysia and I find
myself among millions celebrating
the Hindu Festival of Lights.

I walk the noisy night markets
jammed into closed-off streets
buzzing with yammering
languages alien to my ears.

I tip-toe around dozens
of Rangoli floor mats for sale
awash in minute patterns
of some mystical mandala

and clay pots as luminaria
to line ancient roadways
saffron wafting at every turn
carving spice routes in the air.

A vinegar-faced street vendor
implores me not to miss
tomorrow's rickshaw races.
Maybe I'll do that

then with a finger-snap to reality
I'm back to 46.9 north latitude.
I push to the surface from the deep
end of a dream just in time to hear

Cold enough for ya'? the clerk asks
as I catch myself buying another
sturdy windshield scraper
at the local Ace Hardware.

Bag in hand I step outside
take a deep breath filling my lungs
with all the cold North Dakota
air they can hold.

Where Have All the Clotheslines Gone

oh that ecstasy when crawling into a bed
made fresh with line-dried sheets
corners crimped in wedges from the wind
and whorls left by wooden clothespins

that euphoria inside an envelope smelling
of Fels Naptha and bluing and bleach
muslin against scabby knees
mixed with playground dust

after days of playing hide-and-go-seek
between flat sheets flapping on the line
until a mother scolds us from a kitchen
window propped open on ironing day

The Rabbit

Taking down the last frost-bitten ferns,
the backyard scattered with crisp leaves

painted in hues of jewels blown about
by the season's breezes, I found a rabbit

the one who nibbled off tender vines back in June
and I've kept a jaundiced eye on each day

as I coaxed my clematis back up the trellis.
This one—and its litter-mates—emerged last May

from a nest in the iris patch—wishing I hadn't
forgotten to eliminate the whole lot with my trusty .22

Quick. Clean. Painless.

I filled the birdbath in the frosty dawn—half awake
to something among leaves blustered in the yard but

my first cup of coffee was calling from the kitchen counter.
Later in the glorious warmth of an apple-cider afternoon

there it was again—the young cottontail. This time
on its side, a sky-ward eye open and glazed.

I came closer. Sensing danger it pushed
a limp foot in some primordial attempt to flee.

But its body could not connect to nature's alarm.
In that moment fleas and ants scouted

the furry rise and fall of its chest—
a netherworld between life and death.

I have an obligation. I can't let it suffer.
Damn that ethical code of the prairies.

This could be worse. This could be my beloved
but badly injured horse or my failing old dog.

No, it's a rabbit. Not just any rabbit, mind you.
That clematis-eating varmint!

How far have we come from our prairie ancestors?
Has a manicured suburban life insulated us—

absolved us from nature's grit?
Who are we to rewrite the rules?

Just stop. Trying to gather both courage and resolve,
I let my mind race, buy time: what fate has happened

to this creature? How long had it been there?
Never mind. Was it in pain?

My stomach rose in my throat at its suffering—
Buck up, Woman . . . God, help me do this.

A mind-numbed walk to the shed for the spade.
With pulse pounding in my ears

and a familiar nausea not far behind,
I took aim at the rabbit's neck.

Monday's To-Do List

1.
Vacuum dust bunnies set adrift
by a casual puff of breeze
or by a poltergeist disguised
as clouds in any corner of my house.

> 1.a Note to Self
> An unassuming yellow lab
> whose piles outside
> seem as large as she also need
> a removal project soon.

2.
Take out trash for garbage day
gathered up from waste baskets
full of mostly Kleenex—another species
of small ghosts in any given room.

3.
Hose pine pollen off the porch
heaped in allergy-causing clumps
of yellow dust and dog hair
that manage to plug my nose for days.

4.
Stop avoiding 1.a

Sun Cycle

As earth repeats a circle dance around me
autumn leaves mirror my magic and I
warm your afternoon tea—chase away the frost

> My frigid dawn slides in your morning window
> I spill on your desk where you work
> the lamp shut off for a few short hours

Come outside—we have much to do
Let's chip old ice and greet the finches
shake off darkness and let me warm your bones

> Earth leans so far toward me I
> sneak into your north window—bringing
> chartreuse reflections off tender grass

Summer Trilogy

I

After enduring three years of drought
An unfamiliar rain arrives like a stranger.
I sense we have met somewhere before.

Thinking back, far back. I met this smell
as a child visiting a wooded lake
in Minnesota—a long time from here.

Wet lies thick on the dirt road,
on my skin and in my nose. This mother
and daughter stand at the window.

A promised sandcastle has to wait.
Rain sound settles and soft thunder rolls
from a faraway place and a faded memory.

II

A rare rainy day in summer means a lazy
afternoon to curl up and read.
Showers slow near sunset and the sky
morphs from inky murk to palest gray
then a stroke of peach.

Along the beach above the reed bed,
thinning clouds glimpse
a painter's slop of watercolors
pour dawn onto the lake
just before dusk.

III

Darkness. It must be evening.
I think it's Friday or is it August.
We've looked for the loon for days
He must be gone—the plovers
have left and so have the avocets.
We humans also migrate south
from this place each fall.
Like the prairie birds,
we recover from one summer
waiting for the next.

Epilogue

Late August. Our days here end
when her school begins. Fall presses
on us like some ominous thing.

I knew if we didn't build the sandcastle
I would have regrets some bleak winter night.

When our mansion for imaginary kings
was done, it was unadorned lumps
of sand. The moat a mere sieve.

A tired but happy seven-year-old and no
possible chance for lament when the wind
blows us deep into winter.

Decorations

Pewter nights backdrop
      Waterford crystal mornings
Last summer's faded leaves
      Christmas ornaments
Strung from the emerald maple

Sisterhood of Pines

When we have learned how to listen to trees,
then the brevity and the quickness and the childlike
hastiness of our thoughts achieve an incomparable joy.
~Hermann Hesse

We've been here all along
    we whisper to her in subtle sighs
        in our dialects of ancient conifer and spruce

witnessing more than we dare tell
    beyond doldrums of decades
        sheltering shanty nests of doves in summer

stalwart in winter
    we break northwesterlies
        bed fawns in underskirts of pine straw

murmur in pained sacrifice
    when she steals Christmas boughs
        wounded resin stains her hands

we stand guard and towering
    companioned between yester and yonder
        we sing in our choral voices

Let's go somewhere together
    pine crowns point to the Milky Way
        We've been expecting you

A Meadow for Monarchs

Convince me that you have a seed there,
and I am prepared to expect wonders.
~Henry David Thoreau

As if they are boxelder bugs flaunting
       iridescent tail feathers, I scatter
milkweed seeds in the breeze
       on the sunrise side of the house.

In a couple years I'll look down
       from my second-story hideaway
to find pinked clusters laden with syrup
       intoxicating our dinner guests

dressed in blazing sunset. Wings fan
       like bellows inhaling manna.
My children's children will pass down
       this tale of my insistence

to winter-over a bag of silkened seeds
       in the freezer then broadcast
them by hand across our protected
       patch of virgin prairie

in spite of poison ivy warnings hollered
       at me from the porch. Someday
along with all things spring they will greet
       their velvet-winged visitors.

Surrendering

is not so much giving up
but giving in to the moment

like morning's golden hour before
the rest of the household stirs

when the slant of light
seeps through ancestor grasses

and a grasshopper works
its way up sundried stalks

like finding the disgorged crusty rubble
of mouse bones and fur left below

a gray owl's midnight perch
on gables above our sleeping heads

like the meadowlark's throaty matins
gargled from the fence post

because she is compelled to sing

Acknowledgments and Notes

My appreciation to the editors of these literary journals and publications in which the following poems, sometimes in earlier versions, have appeared:

Evening Street Review: "The Rabbit"

Faith and Form and AIA ND Architect: "Lesson in the Wine Cellar"

Flying South Literary Magazine, Poetry Competition, Winston-Salem Writers: "Pendulum of Ordinary Time"

Midwest Review, Great Midwest Poetry Contest, Semi-Finalist: "Surrendering"

Kallisto Press, Julia Darling Memorial Poetry Prize, Finalist: "Grasslands"

The MacGuffin: "A Force of Nature," "Coyote Comes Calling," and "Mistress of Millennia"

North Dakota Quarterly: "When the Water Recedes"

Pasque Petals, South Dakota State Poetry Society: "Yellow on the Willow," "Meadow for Monarchs," and "On the Prairie You Never Get Used to the Wind"

Pendora Magazine: "Dear Kate" appears under the title "McCoy Hall Roommates"

*Plainsong*s: "Face in Her Phone"

Poeming Pigeon COSMOS Anthology, The Poetry Box: "Clouds on Parade"

Poetic License Press UNSEEN Anthology: "It's All the Rage"

Prairie Fire: "Memory Care"

Sanskrit Literary Arts Magazine: "Displacement Postponed," "Clouds on Parade," and "Edge of Dismantling"

Straight Forward Poetry: "Pear Tree on Highland Acres Road"

The following poems appeared in my debut chapbook, *Destiny Manifested*, published by NDSU Press, 2018:

"49th Parallel"
"Bakken Roughneck"
"Shuttle to Rockport by the Sea"
"Standing Ground"

Additional craft notes on form: "Ode to Barbwire" (Bivalve); "Owling" (Tanka); "Standing Ground" (Pantoum); "Roadside Memorial" (Double Tanka); "Bakken Roughneck" (Sestina); "Face in Her Phone" (Acrostic).

My profound gratitude to these individuals who encourage, read, humor, and cajole me: my daughter, Stacy Staiger Krumwiede, my son-in-law, Mike Krumwiede, my grandsons Elliot, Archer, and Owen; my friends and readers Carol Kapsner and Bertrand Vogelweide, O.S.B.; my "Poet Sisters" Susan Coultrap-McQuin, Ellen Lager, and Lynne Lampe; instructors and mentors Amie Whittemore, Kevin Pilkington, and LouAnn Muhm; Dr. Tom Isern and, especially, Dr. Suzzanne Kelley.

About the Author

Bonnie Larson Staiger is a North Dakota Associate Poet Laureate and a North Dakota Humanities Scholar. Her second book, *In Plains Sight*, follows close on the heels of her success with *Manifest Destiny*, winner of the 2018 Poetry of the Plains and Prairie Prize from North Dakota State University Press and recognized as Distinguished Favorite in the Category of Poetry for the 2019 Independent Press Award. She recently received awards from *Flying South Literary Magazine* and The MacGuffin's Best of the Year Anthology, and she was a finalist for the Julia Darling Poetry Prize and the Great Midwest Poetry Prize.

Bonnie is immersed in the poetry world and has studied with notable poets Rick Barot, Richard Blanco, Kevin Pilkington, Ross Gay, Ilya Kaminsky, Tom Sleigh, and Kathleen Norris. She focuses her writing on life in the plains, not just in *In Plains Sight*, but in all of her work. Bonnie has held multiple officer leadership positions in North Dakota and National societies, and she is the founding president of the North Dakota State Poetry Society—a chapter of a national federation that publishes and promotes poetry and hosts festivals and writing workshops.

Bonnie lives in Bismarck, ND, and often writes of the poignant subtleties of life on the northern plains of the American West as well as a world view observed from and shaped by that place. Her current projects and programs can be found at https://bonniestaiger.com and on Twitter at @BonnieStaiger.

About the Press

North Dakota State University Press (NDSU Press) exists to stimulate and coordinate interdisciplinary regional scholarship. These regions include the Red River Valley, the state of North Dakota, the plains of North America (comprising both the Great Plains of the United States and the prairies of Canada), and comparable regions of other continents. We publish peer reviewed regional scholarship shaped by national and international events and comparative studies.

Neither topic nor discipline limits the scope of NDSU Press publications. We consider manuscripts in any field of learning. We define our scope, however, by a regional focus in accord with the press's mission. Generally, works published by NDSU Press address regional life directly, as the subject of study. Such works contribute to scholarly knowledge of region (that is, discovery of new knowledge) or to public consciousness of region (that is, dissemination of information, or interpretation of regional experience). Where regions abroad are treated, either for comparison or because of ties to those North American regions of primary concern to the press, the linkages are made plain. For nearly three-quarters of a century, NDSU Press has published substantial trade books, but the line of publications is not limited to that genre. We also publish textbooks (at any level), reference books, anthologies, reprints, papers, proceedings, and monographs. The press also considers works of poetry or fiction, provided they are established regional classics or they promise to assume landmark or reference status for the region. We select biographical or autobiographical works carefully for their prospective contribution to regional knowledge and culture. All publications, in whatever genre, are of such quality and substance as to embellish the imprint of NDSU Press.

We changed our imprint to North Dakota State University Press in January 2016. Prior to that, and since 1950, we published as the North Dakota Institute for Regional Studies Press. We continue to operate under the umbrella of the North Dakota Institute for Regional Studies, located at North Dakota State University.